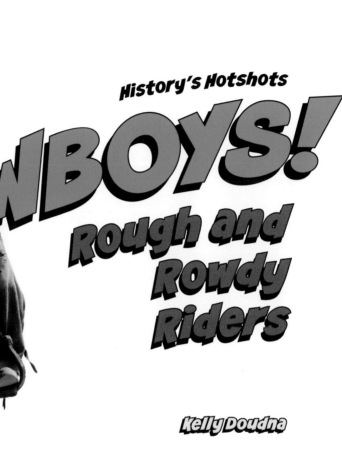

History's Hotshots

COWBOYS!

Rough and Rowdy Riders

Kelly Doudna

Checkerboard Library

An Imprint of Abdo Publishing
abdopublishing.com

abdopublishing.com

Published by Abdo Publishing, a division of ABDO, PO Box 398166, Minneapolis, Minnesota 55439. Copyright © 2018 by Abdo Consulting Group, Inc. International copyrights reserved in all countries. No part of this book may be reproduced in any form without written permission from the publisher. Checkerboard Library™ is a trademark and logo of Abdo Publishing.

Printed in the United States of America, North Mankato, Minnesota
102017
012018

THIS BOOK CONTAINS RECYCLED MATERIALS

Design: Kelly Doudna, Mighty Media, Inc.
Production: Mighty Media, Inc.
Editor: Jessie Alkire
Cover Photograph: Shutterstock
Design Elements: Shutterstock
Interior Photographs: Alamy, pp. 8 (middle), 11, 13, 19, 27; Flickr, p. 25; iStockphoto, pp. 4-5, 8 (bottom), 17, 29; Mighty Media, Inc., pp. 7, 23; Shutterstock, pp. 1, 7, 15, 23; Wikimedia Commons, pp. 6, 8 (top), 9, 10, 21, 22

Publisher's Cataloging-in-Publication Data

Names: Doudna, Kelly, author.
Title: Cowboys! rough and rowdy riders / by Kelly Doudna.
Other titles: Rough and rowdy riders
Description: Minneapolis, Minnesota : Abdo Publishing, 2018. | Series: History's hotshots |
    Includes online resources and index.
Identifiers: LCCN 2017944063 | ISBN 9781532112713 (lib.bdg.) | ISBN 9781532150432 (ebook)
Subjects: LCSH: Cowboys--Juvenile literature. | Frontier and pioneer life--Juvenile literature. |
    West (U.S.) -- Social life and customs--Juvenile literature. | United States, West--Juvenile
    literature.
Classification: DDC 978.02--dc23
LC record available at https://lccn.loc.gov/2017944063

Contents

RIDING the RANGE

Your hands blister as you grip the leather of your horse's reins. The animal kicks up dust as you guide it toward a runaway calf at full speed. Within seconds, you've thrown your lariat around the calf's neck. You catch your breath as you guide the animal back to the herd.

The cattle herd is your responsibility. You work with ten other men, but you are in charge. You have spent the past two months driving the 3,000 cattle along the open range. You have traveled nearly 1,000 miles (1,609 km) across the American West.

Along the way, you have defended the herd from wild animals and cattle **rustlers**. You've calmed the herd when it was frightened by bad weather. You've even raced around the herd in circles to stop the cattle from stampeding.

With the runaway calf returned to its herd, you urge your horse forward. You are nearing the railroad where the cattle will be shipped and sold. You are tired, but you are ready to begin another adventure. Your skills are put to the test every day. But you can handle it. You are an American cowboy!

Who Are Cowboys?

The cowboy of the American West can trace his roots to Spain in the **Middle Ages.** There, large agricultural estates were known as haciendas. Cattle ranches were one kind of hacienda. Cattle were overseen by men on horseback called vaqueros.

Italian explorer Christopher Columbus crossed the Atlantic Ocean in 1492. His trip was supported by Spain. Spanish explorers soon followed. They settled many areas in the Americas. The settlers brought cattle and horses with them. They established haciendas in new territories. One of the largest territories was Mexico.

In 1776, the American colonies had declared independence from England. People in the United States looked westward with the desire to expand. Farming and ranching were common ways to make a living.

Hacienda *usually referred to a large estate. Some haciendas were plantations, while others were mines or factories.*

UNITED STATES

ATLANTIC OCEAN

MEXICO

GULF OF MEXICO

PACIFIC OCEAN

COWBOY LANDS

MAP KEY

Areas of open range

The Mexican government encouraged Americans to settle in Texas to promote trade. However, conflict soon broke out. Texas declared its independence from Mexico in 1836 and later became a US state in 1845. Then, the **Mexican-American War** began in 1846 in a disagreement over territory.

The war ended in 1848 with Mexico losing one-third of its territory. Many Mexican ranchers fled the territory during the war and returned to Mexico. They left much of their livestock behind. Five million cattle roamed the United States. The **heyday** of the American cowboy was about to begin!

Timeline

1492–1500s The Spanish cross the Atlantic and settle in the Americas. They bring cattle and horses with them and build ranches.

1846 The **Mexican-American War** begins. Mexican ranchers leave their livestock behind. The age of the cowboy begins.

1867 A new **railhead** opens in Abilene, Kansas. Cowboys drive 36,000 cattle to Abilene along a route that becomes known as the Chisholm Trail.

1876 Cowboy Nat Love works on a cattle drive to the Dakota Territory. He wins a rodeo in Deadwood and earns the nickname "Deadwood Dick."

1880s–1890s Railroad expansions and harsh winters lead to decreased demand for cowboys.

1900s Rodeos grow in popularity and become serious competitions for modern cowboys to show off their skills.

1930s–1940s Western movies become popular in the United States. These movies create the modern, often incorrect, image of the American cowboy.

Deadwood Dick

Nat Love was an African-American cowboy. Love was born into slavery in Davidson County, Tennessee, in 1854. Soon after slavery was abolished in 1865, Love headed west.

Love worked on cattle drives in Texas and Arizona. He became an expert at shooting guns. He claimed to have fought off **rustlers**.

In 1876, Love went on a cattle drive to the Dakota Territory. On July 4, he entered a rodeo in the territory's city of Deadwood. Love won the rodeo, earning the nickname "Deadwood Dick." The next year, Love was captured by Native Americans. He later escaped on a stolen horse.

In 1889, Love got married and left the cowboy life behind. He got a job working for a railroad. Love settled down in California. He wrote a book about his life in 1907. The book detailed Love's adventures. It cemented Love's legendary cowboy status.

Driven by Economics

In the mid-1800s, more settlers moved west. They hired cowboys to round up cattle and look after their ranches. Cowboys kept herds together. They protected cattle from being stolen by cattle **rustlers** and Native Americans.

Most ranchers kept only enough cattle to provide for their own needs. If ranchers had extra meat or hides, they sold these parts within their local area. Animals were abundant, but the market for animal products had not yet developed.

Change came with the **American Civil War** in 1861. Hungry troops created an increased demand for beef and other meat products. The war ended in 1865. Soon after, industrialists opened meatpacking plants.

Cowboys were usually single men in their late teens or early 20s. These men had to be healthy and strong to withstand harsh conditions on the range.

Cowboys of Color

Settlers from the southern United States took their slaves with them when they moved west. The **census** of 1860 showed that African Americans made up one-third of the Texas population. Then, the **American Civil War** broke out. White landowners left to fight in the war. The slaves stayed behind to work the ranches. They acquired the same skills as white cowboys.

After the Civil War ended, the African-American cowboys were free men. Working as a cowboy was one of the few jobs open to men of color. One in four cowboys was African American. Many more cowboys had Mexican heritage. Men worked as equals tending the herd, so there was little **discrimination**.

Ranchers could sell cattle for much higher prices in the North. In Chicago, Illinois, ranchers were paid up to $60 per animal. This was ten times what cattle were worth in Texas. Cowboys were called upon to drive herds to places where the cattle could be shipped to market.

Ride to the Railroad

To get their herds to market in the North, ranchers first had to get them to a **railhead.** American railroads had been spreading from the east coast to the Midwest. Sedalia, Missouri, was the nearest rail station to Texas.

Cowboys attempted to drive a large herd toward Sedalia in 1866. However, they were blocked in Kansas. Farmers in Kansas were afraid the Texas cattle would transmit cattle fever to their herds. This was a sickness that could cause death for cattle. The Texas cattle didn't get sick from the fever, but they carried ticks that spread the disease.

In 1867, a new railhead opened in Abilene, Kansas. This new location was west of Kansas farmland. It was closer to Texas and had a cattle shipping facility. Cowboys successfully drove 36,000 cattle to Abilene that year. The route they took became known as the Chisholm Trail. It was about 800 miles (1,287 km) long.

Railroad lines continued to expand. Over the next ten years, they

Hotshot Fact

As a young man, US president Theodore Roosevelt worked as a cowboy. He learned many skills that he later used as president, including quick decision making.

A monument called "On the Chisholm Trail" was created by sculptor Paul Moore. The monument is displayed at the Chisholm Trail Heritage Center in Oklahoma.

spread westward as demand for beef grew. A new **railhead** in Dodge City, Kansas, shipped 500,000 cattle in 1877. Dodge City called itself the "cowboy capital of the world."

CHAPTER 4

Rapid Decline

The **heyday** of the long-range cattle drive was short-lived. As quickly as it had risen in importance, the need for cowboys disappeared. New inventions were one factor that decreased the need for cowboys.

The invention of **barbed wire** in 1874 led to the fall of long-range cattle driving. Suddenly, landowners could fence off their property. The fencing controlled where cattle could roam and graze. Fewer cowboys were needed to tend herds.

Weather was another factor that affected cowboy populations. The winter of 1886 to 1887 was cold and harsh. Cowboys tried their best to keep the cattle warm and healthy, but millions of cattle died. The cattle that lived were thin and sickly. They were worth far less at market. Many ranchers lost money and couldn't afford cowboys.

By the 1890s, rail lines connected most of the country. More meatpacking plants had been built closer to ranching areas. Long cattle drives were no longer needed to reach **railheads** or markets. Shipment by rail became the standard way to move cattle. The age of the cowboy was over.

Railcars used to transport livestock were often called cattle cars. These cars had covered roofs and slatted sides. They could hold 20,000 to 30,000 pounds (9,072 to 13,608 kg).

CHAPTER 5

Cattle Round-Up

During the height of the cowboy era, a typical herd numbered around 3,000 cattle. Ten or more cowboys were needed to manage a herd this size. Cattle grazed on the open range for much of the year. From time to time, the cowboys would move the cattle to a new grazing area. But most of the time, cattle lived with little human interference.

This all changed in the springtime. It was time for the cowboys to round up their cattle. This was no small feat! Cowboys drove their horses around, behind, and even directly into huge herds to get their cattle to move. The cowboys then directed their herds to ranches.

Cowboys had many tough tasks on the ranch. One was branding calves. A brand was an identifying mark **unique** to each ranch. A cowboy heated a piece of iron in the shape of the mark and burned it into a calf's hide. The resulting scar allowed cowboys to identify and count members of their herd.

A herd only needed a few bulls to breed for the next generation. So, cowboys **castrated** most of the male calves. The calves would then be allowed to grow to market size.

Rounding up cattle could mean hours of high-speed riding and roping!

Cowboys also separated out the animals meant for market. These cattle would be driven to the nearest **railhead** to be shipped and sold. The rest of the herd returned to the range.

Driving the Herd

Driving a herd of cattle to a **railhead** required additional crew members. These included a cook, a horse wrangler, and a trail boss. In addition to making food, the cook drove the wagon. He usually had some medical skills as well. The horse wrangler was often very young. This junior cowboy managed the extra horses during the drive. The trail boss was in charge of the whole drive.

The pace of the drive had to be managed carefully. Cowboys found that 15 miles (24 km) per day was the ideal distance. Cattle then had enough time to graze and rest. At this pace, a drive could take months!

A cowboy on a drive had to be ready for action at a moment's notice. If he wasn't, it could mean life or death! Cowboys were sometimes fired upon by hostile farmers or Native Americans. Cowboys also had to be **vigilant** against cattle **rustlers**. The weather could also be life-threatening.

Hotshot Fact

The sound of voices was calming to cattle. A cowboy on night watch would sing to the herd as he made his rounds. These songs became the roots of country-western music.

Cowboys earned about $25 to $40 a month for their work. They also received food as payment.

Cowboys lived outdoors day and night. There was no shelter from storms or extreme heat.

There was always the risk of a stampede. If this happened, cowboys drove the herd in a circle. The cattle eventually grew tired and stopped running. But this could take hours!

CHAPTER 7

Magnificent Mustangs

A cowboy's horse was his most valuable possession. The ideal horse was small and compact. It was also smart and stayed calm under pressure. It knew how to work around cattle. The best horses for the job had what cowboys called a "cow sense." This was the animal's ability to expect the movements of the cattle.

Horses had been extinct in North America since the **Ice Age**. The Spanish settlers of the 1500s brought horses with them. Like cattle, many horses were left behind during conflict. These wild horses became known as mustangs.

Cowboys who rounded up and tamed mustangs were called "mustang runners." These horses were used on the ranch or sold. Because their work was so tiring, cowboys would often ride three or four horses each day. This gave the horses time to rest. But the cowboys were in the saddle all day!

A cowboy's saddle was his other vital possession. Many cowboys had custom saddles. The design had developed from that used by vaqueros. The front and back of the saddle were high. This created a deep, secure seat. A wide

One definition of cowboys in the 1800s was "anybody with guts and a horse."

stirrup hung down each side. This design provided maximum comfort for both the cowboy and his horse.

Cowboy Couture

Cowboys needed clothing that covered and protected their bodies from the elements. They wore tall boots that protected their lower legs. The boots had pointed toes that easily fit through **stirrups**. The boots' high heels securely wedged cowboys' feet in the stirrups.

Leather chaps provided upper leg protection while riding. They kept a cowboy's jeans from snagging on heavy brush or thorns. Chaps also protected jeans from tearing while a cowboy did rough work with cattle and mustangs.

The cowboy hat was adapted from wide-brimmed hats worn by Mexican vaqueros. The brim shielded the wearer from the sun and rain. The cowboy hat also had a high crown

Cowboys often wore jeans or other pants made of a thick material, such as canvas. These pants were sturdy and long-lasting.

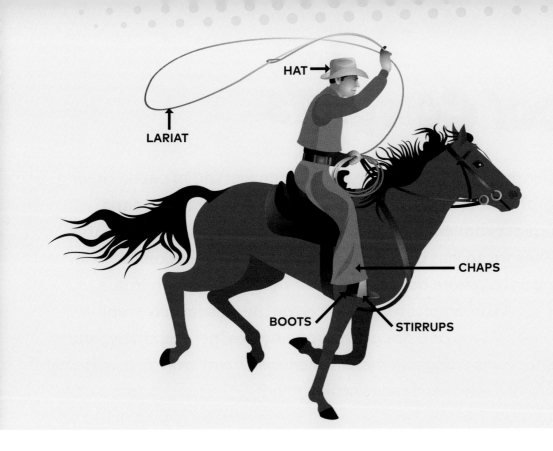

HAT

LARIAT

CHAPS

BOOTS

STIRRUPS

to keep the wearer's head cool. A cowboy could even carry water in his hat!

A cowboy always had a rope called a lariat on hand to catch stray cattle. The lariat was made of twisted or braided rawhide or leather. It had a small loop at one end. The cowboy threaded the free end through the loop. He threw this larger loop around an animal's neck or leg. Then, he pulled the loop tight to catch his target!

Cool Cowgirls

Historians don't think many women worked in cattle driving professionally. However, Western women had an early equality advantage over other women in the United States. They faced less **discrimination** in many aspects of life. They also took more active roles in society and in the home.

Women often worked on ranches, especially small ones. Wives and daughters rode horses, herded cattle, and shot guns alongside men. When men went to war, it was the women who kept the ranches going.

WILD WEST SHOWS

Many cowboys performed in rodeos. These are events where cowboys show off their riding and roping talents. Rodeos led to the creation of Wild West shows. These shows presented cattle-ranching skills and other tricks in a circus-like setting.

Women were prominent performers in Wild West shows. Annie Oakley was one performer. She became famous for her shooting skills. Fanny Sperry Steele was a champion **bronco** rider.

Women worked just as hard on ranches as men did. They would often go to bed near midnight and then get up at 4 o'clock in the morning to start working again!

The term "cowgirl" was first used in 1884. But Lucille Mulhall gave the word meaning. From childhood, she was an expert rider and roper and performed in her family's Wild West show. In 1913, Mulhall formed her own show. In 1916, she produced a rodeo.

Making a Myth

Cowgirls and cowboys alike have inspired many myths in American **culture.** These myths have been explored in Western shows, novels, and films since the late 1800s. However, these representations of cowboy life are often sensational and incorrect.

Dime novels were popular between about 1860 and 1915. These were dramatic tales often based on real events. An author focused on an interesting, real person. Then, true events of the person's life were exaggerated. Cowboys were popular dime novel subjects. Cowboy **duels** with guns were largely an invention of the dime novel.

Hollywood also played a large role in spreading cowboy myths. Western movies were popular entertainment in the 1930s and 1940s. But they did not show realistic cowboy life. In these movies, cowboys were often shown as lone gunmen who had little time for ranching. These characters often had shootouts with one another and with Native Americans.

In reality, cowboys seldom worked alone. Teamwork was vital when controlling a herd of thousands of cattle.

John Wayne was a popular actor who often played cowboy characters. He starred in 142 films, many of them Westerns!

And while cowboys did carry guns, they most often used these weapons to defend cattle from predators and **rustlers**. Armed conflicts between cowboys and Native Americans occurred, but they were rare.

Cowboys Today

Although they don't look like the cowboys of Hollywood, cowboys still exist today! But they still need the same skills around the ranch. Rodeos remain a way to compete and show off those skills.

In the 1820s and 1830s, rodeos were very informal. When a cattle drive was over, cowboys tested their skills and competed with one another. This was a friendly competition. It also provided entertainment after a tiring day on the range.

In the early 1900s, rodeos gained greater popularity and competition became more serious. Today, cowboys can earn a living as rodeo competitors. These performers compete in events such as **bronco** riding, cattle wrestling, and bull riding. Women compete separately in events such as barrel racing.

The golden age of cowboys is long past. But it was an important part of American history. The myth of the cowboy continues to fascinate people. And as long as large ranches exist, the need for cowboys on horseback will remain!

Many cowboys who participate in rodeos consider themselves professional athletes. They think of rodeo as a sport that combines both performance and contest.

Glossary

American Civil War – the war between the Northern and Southern states from 1861 to 1865.

barbed wire – wire that has sharp points.

bronco – an untamed horse of western North America.

castrate – to perform a procedure that prevents reproduction.

census – a count of the population of a certain area.

culture – the customs, arts, and tools of a nation or a people at a certain time.

discrimination (dihs-krih-muh-NAY-shuhn) – unfair treatment, often based on race, religion, or gender.

duel – a formal fight conducted by two people following a set of rules.

heyday – a period of great success or popularity.

Ice Age – a period of time between 1.8 million years ago and 11,500 years ago that includes several ice ages. An ice age is a time when thick ice sheets cover large areas of land.

Mexican-American War – A war fought between the United States and Mexico from 1846 to 1848.

Middle Ages – a period in European history that lasted from about 500 CE to about 1500 CE.

railhead – a point on a railroad where traffic begins or ends.

rustle – to steal, usually cattle. One who steals cattle is a rustler.

stirrup – one of a pair of loops or rings hanging from a saddle. Stirrups are used as footholds to help in mounting and riding.

unique (yoo-NEEK) – being the only one of its kind.

vigilant – alert to signs of danger.

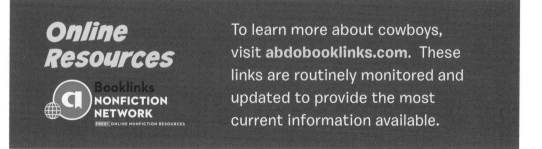

Index